Am I Too Sexy?

Stan Pearson II, MBA

www.stanpearson.com
www.amitoosexy.com
www.everydaysexypodcast.com
www.simplyspeakuniversity.com
www.leadfollowormove.com

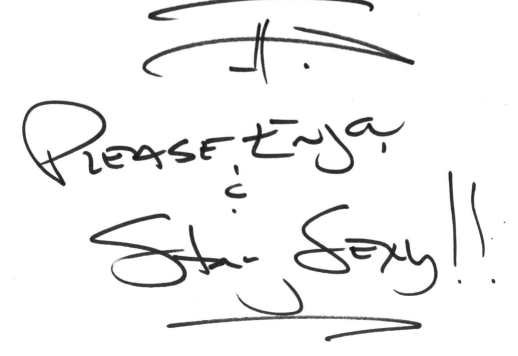

Please Enjoy!

Stay Sexy!!

MOTIVATE AND INSPIRE OTHERS!

BOOK ME TO SPEAK

TO YOUR ORGANIZATION, SCHOOL, BUSINESS OR MASTERMIND

"SHARE THIS BOOK"

SPECIAL QUANTITY DISCOUNTS

5- 20 Books	$15.95
21-99 Books	$14.95
100-499 Books	$13.95
500-999 Books	$11.95
1000+ Books	$8.95

TO PLACE AN ORDER CONTACT:
888.498.7826
STAN@STANPEARSON.COM

#FINDYOURSEXY
#AMITOOSEXY
#EVERYDAYSEXY
#CONTROLYOURFEED

DEDICATION

If you are reading this, it's because you've heard me speak, seen Am I TOO Sexy? apparel or have randomly passed by someone who has come in contact with the Am I TOO Sexy? brand and wondered what it all means. This book is dedicated to anyone who has ever felt less than, lacked confidence for any reason or simply wanted to know if ANYONE in this world understands what it means to be imperfect besides them. If you spend your life trying to please everyone else, you will never be able to please the person most important, which is you. This book is dedicated to anyone who has ever felt like no one loved them, no one cared for them or everyone has ignored them. This book is dedicated to YOU! We're not so different after all are we? If you have come in contact with this book, it was not by accident. When you finish it, please pass this feeling, notion, explanation and book along. The world could use it! This book is dedicated to the world that needs it. We don't have to be perfect, we just have to try to be better today than we were yesterday!

CONTENTS

ACKNOWLEDGMENTS

I would like to acknowledge the students, staff & professionals I have come in contact with while on tour through 45 states in addition to Mexico, Spain, Canada, The U.S Virgin Islands & the British Virgin Islands. Every person I meet inspires me to continue my journey in life as imperfectly perfect as it is. I know I am not alone. Continue to know yourself, love yourself & be yourself. I also acknowledge the people responsible for bringing me to this point in my life; my parents, Stanley and Patricia Pearson and my sisters, Vanoy and Stephanie, who continue to push me to strive, grow and share a message that the world needs to hear. They inspire me daily and are the reason I have made it this far. They remind me that you get out of life what you put into it. As my mom often says, when the dream is big enough, the "facts" don't count!

1. SEXINESS DEFINED

The other day I accompanied my good friend to her high school reunion. She had not seen her former classmates for what seemed an eternity. I was playing the role of the fake boyfriend (a role I played quite well —an Oscar lieth in wait for me!), so she wouldn't have to endure the embarrassment of admitting ten years down the line, she was still single.

Thank goodness for name tags, because none of the attendants could recognize each other. After all the fake smiles, insincere greetings and feigned excitement to see each other, the large cluster broke up and

I found myself in a smaller group whose sole purpose seemed to be discussing everybody at the party.

The conversations went like this: "Did you see Hannah? She has become too skinny, I bet she's anorexic." Another member of this group would gladly join in. "Honey, that's nothing. Did you see Pete? He has gained like twice his former body size. He used to be the sexy quarterback. How could he let himself get so huge?!"

I clearly recall one particularly nasty lady saying "Remember Ruby? As in, No–Booby Ruby? There is no way her chest could have become that big. I heard she got a boob job from some quack. No surprise then that her top half is too big for her body."

All the while I remained silent. After all, I was here on the pretext of being someone's boyfriend. I did not want to draw attention to myself. However, I couldn't help but ask myself: on what basis do these people judge someone as either acceptable or unacceptable? Everyone seemed to have something so wrong with them that they could not fit in.

This event (a type which I vowed to never ever attend in the future) began the prompting in my mind: what does it take for an individual to be considered sexy? Curious, I undertook an extremely unscientific poll among some friends and colleagues. I asked them to choose which of five statements they felt was closest to what they believe being sexy is about. The results speak for themselves:

35% agreed with this statement: "To be sexy means to ooze **confidence**; to be so comfortable in your own skin and personality that you develop an unshakeable self-confidence that everyone can notice about you. With this confidence comes a certain kind of subtle cockiness and surety about someone that just makes you want to (insert naughty thought here). Sexiness is undoubtedly confidence."

28% ticked this statement as being the accurate definition of sexy; "**Looks and Body**! Looks and Body! Looks and Body! Being sexy is having all the right curves in all the right places, having the right abs and being so good-looking that everybody can't help but notice you whenever you pass by. Ultimately, sexiness is about killer looks and a killer body that makes one want to (again, insert naughty thought here) whenever they see you." Sexiness is all in the physical.

21% (all females!) couldn't agree more with this: "**Cash** is king, baby! Nothing makes a man sexier than a bulge in his pocket. When a man has money, he can buy all things made that represent sexiness – flashy cars, an enviable mansion, designer scents and clothing ...you name it! A man who has made it in life is so sexy, he opens his wallet and I just want to open my (you know where this is going!). Ultimately, money is sexy."

11% felt this statement spoke to them "It's all in the **spirit**. Someone with zest for life is definitely sexy...you know the type: very adventurous, spontaneous, optimistic, happy and humorous and just so full of life. This person is like a breath of fresh air in a polluted city and spending time with them just turns you on. Such a person never worries about the future and lives for today rather fearlessly. Such a spirit-that is the epitome of sexiness."

The minority 5% were more inclined to choose this statement "Sexiness is all about wit and **intelligence**. Smart is the new sexy and nothing turns me on faster than a man/woman with brains. Such a person is not easily deceived and can get themselves out of any bad situation using their brain power. Sex starts in the mind, and for me this means that intelligence is indeed sexiness."

This fascinating poll brought out one thing: the sexiness hierarchy starts with **confidence,** followed by **looks, money, spirit and smarts.**

It's a little more complicated in real life, however. All of those attributes might matter to one degree or another, but in the end, everybody has a different idea and understanding of the term sexy. When people meet an individual who doesn't match their understanding of "sexy", they are quick to label them as too much of something, which disqualifies them from fitting in the sexy category. The poll showed me what people care about, but it also made me realize what they cast aside is just as important. This insight was the birth of the "TOO" factor.

Think about it. How many times in your life have you been told that you're "too much of something" to fit in? Look at this table and tick where you have been described as possessing the "TOO" factor:

The "TOO" Table			
Tall	Loud	Creepy	Sarcastic
Short	Fat	Weird	Sweet

Plain	Skinny	White	Holy Joe
Fancy	Geeky	Black	Blonde
Quiet	Dumb	Gangster	Nice

Society has commanded that we all fit into neat little boxes: a certain weight, height, and figure. Failure to fit in leads to automatic social rejection and a life filled with insecurities and low self-esteem. Unfortunately, as you will see, there are too many boxes—all too narrow. The result is that practically everyone suffers from self-doubt and low self-worth.

This is tragic and ironic. If we take a moment to think about it, the things that make us unique are what make us special. You're not special because you talk or look like everybody else. You're special because there is something you do which no one else can do. This is **your TOO factor.** If we all aimed at fitting into the societal boxes, wouldn't we be more like bad clones? Can you imagine living in a world where everybody is exactly the same? It would be like being stuck in Stepford Wives for infinity!

My wheels were turning. When we don't fit into predefined boxes, we get rejected. But the things that make us not fit in make us stand out. It hit me that every single person who is remembered the world over; every single person who is some form of celebrity has the TOO sexy factor, and that's what got them to where they are today.

Let's examine a few famous people to prove this point.

1. I'm TOO sexy because I'm...GEEKY

You think you're too much of a geek to be cool? Think again. Most of the innovation in the world—most of its

technological progress, from the wheel to the space shuttle and beyond—have happened because of geeks.

Which geek do we all know took the world by storm and now has billions of dollars to his name? That's right, Bill Gates. First, he revolutionized the personal computer industry and now he's using his analytical approach to become the most effective philanthropist ever. Do you see anyone laughing or making fun of this geek?

If you are considered a geek and feel like you're kept at the border of every social event, do not despair. Since when is being a geek or weird a bad thing? Embrace YOURSELF. Think: What would Bill Gates do? He would probably take that time to plan something the world has never seen before and be compensated for it.

Geeks have just the right attributes to not only survive, but to thrive. They have the curiosity to become experts in the subject they are passionate about, and the drive to turn it into something bigger than it had started out with.

Geeky people often end up being the bosses of the "cool" people. In other words, if you're a geek out there, your turn to shine is on its way! When you land the challenging, high-paying job and have people coming to you for your opinion, you will soon be thanking your lucky stars for your Geekiness TOO factor!

1. I'm TOO sexy because I'm...DUMB

Perhaps you have been labeled dumb by your peers, teachers or anybody else in your social circle. You know who else was labeled dumb? Mr. E=MC2 himself, a.k.a Albert Einstein.

Einstein took a long time to learn to speak. Ironically, he was labeled slow; a teacher once even told him (the man who later became the most renowned scientist in the world) that he would never amount to anything. If I were that person, I would perpetually bow my head in shame.

Some people are labeled dumb because they don't think the way others do. Seeing the world differently is exactly what made Einstein one of the greatest thinkers of all time. Because he was able to see past the preconceived notions of his time, he challenged commonly held principles and showed the world that thinking differently hardly equates to stupidity.

We don't have to be Einstein to shake things up, however. The next time someone calls you dumb, you should ask yourself if it's because you can't understand something, or because they aren't able to understand your vision. Yes, thinking the same way everyone else does might help you fit in better, but what would you be giving up for that "privilege"?

Every great innovation—in science and society—started because someone took the time to look at the same old things in a different way. Remember, the next time someone calls you dumb, smile because your unique way of seeing things may lead you to discover the next greatest thing.

3) Am I TOO sexy because I am...BIG

There are a myriad of reasons people weigh what they do. Poor eating and exercising habits can sabotage  people at both ends of the spectrum—making someone frighteningly thin and flaccid or dangerously hefty and out of shape. To have a truly balanced life, it is important to eat right and exercise enough. But we all know people who can shovel food away without gaining weight, and people who count every calorie and still can't shed that extra weight.

Some people, because of genetics tend to be larger bodied, regardless of their diet and exercise regimen. If this is you, you should not be filled with gloom because of your size. Yes, people judge by appearance. But even in the shallowest place on earth—Hollywood—one fantastic woman has proven you don't have to be anorexic to have the 'it' factor.

Look at the lovely lady to your left—Queen Latifah. She raps, she acts and she knows how to be both a home-girl and a lady. In other words, she has mad talent! Yet she is not your run-of-the-mill, pint-sized celebrity that Hollywood churns out these days. Having a fuller body has never prevented her from living out her dreams. In fact, this is one woman who proves that confidence is indeed the sexiest element! Even a multimillion dollar cosmetics company has realized this—and compensated her beautifully to tie her face to their products.

In short, having a large frame is not something to be ashamed of. Your worst enemy in this case is yourself. Carry your weight with pride and confidence and you will be pleasantly surprised to find out you have many admirers just waiting for you to notice them.

4) Am I TOO sexy because I am...WHITE/BLACK

Marshall Mathers—a.k.a. Eminem—might have two names, but this guy needs no introduction. Not because he was born with a silver spoon or given any advantages, but because he paved a path for himself despite the obstacles his race caused him.

I wonder what life was like for Eminem growing up as a white kid in a black neighborhood. More likely than not, when he first started rapping, he was tormented by other kids who spit out phrases like "You can't rap, you're white." Yet he loved to rap and had a raw talent that he was willing to work at. Imagine if he had let those "haters" decide his fate for him? Today he has proven his worth as a rapper many times over, regardless of his skin color.

Race is something we can't change: we are simply born into it. Yes, different groups of people may tend to behave one way or another. But just because you don't fit into preconceived notions, should you try to change who you are? Of course not! Period.

Remember, when you step from one cultural stream to another, you are bringing insights and ideas that other people might not be able to bring. You can have twice the perspective of most people. Don't listen to the naysayers; just use the fact that race is only skin-deep to your advantage.

You can create or master something wonderful from an unexpected starting point. Eminem raps and Tiger Woods plays golf. Next time someone puts you down because of your race, just remember you're TOO sexy for that!

5) Am I TOO sexy because I am ...WEIRD

Weird. That's how folks describe people they don't understand. In other words, it's yet another societal label, not anything that has to do with the "weirdos" themselves.

This man is Alfred Matthew Yankovic, better known by his fans as Weird Al Yankovic, a parody musician and actor. Everything about him is "weird"...his clothes, his hair-do, and particularly his hilarious and over-the-top lyrics. But he has managed to wrap his TOO weird factor in a comical and lovable manner, and cash in on it.

Alfred learned to play the accordion early in life, and was two grades ahead of his peers. He wasn't into sports or the same social scene as his classmates. He was "weird", and everyone knew it. But weird hardly means bad; it just means different. And different gives you the opportunity to stand out -and standing out is what lets you make waves.

In that "weird" brain of his, Al Yankovic was dreaming up different ways of doing things. His weird nature is what got him into musical parody. Now he's made a ton of money having fun and being clever. Clearly, being weird has potential. Use it!

6) Am I TOO sexy because I am ...TALL

 We all recognize this beautiful talk-show host, Tyra Banks. Tyra openly admits growing up she was the gawky, gangly kid who was almost literally heads above her peers. This made her feel different and even un-comfortable. It's hard to literally stand out from the crowd. But did she slouch to try to fit in with everyone else? Nope. She held her head high and before you knew it, she was asked to enter the glamorous model-ing world.

Even during her early days of success, she felt like she stood out—in a bad way. But her height allowed her to do something she enjoyed and to get paid for it. Tyra went much further, though; she knew her height had opened doors, and she was smart and passionate enough to leverage it to even greater success. Tyra wouldn't be where she is today if she were only a tall beauty—even though that's what popped out to people at first glance.

Tyra knew she wasn't limited by her TOO factor—she embraced her height. At the same time, she also knew she wasn't defined by it; being tall helped her get into modeling, but being Tyra let her become a talk show host, producer, and author.

See why your TOO factor is very important? Play it right and what the world perceives as "different" may actually be the key to unlocking your success!

7) Am I TOO sexy because I am ...A TOMBOY

One of the things that most stands out about her is how little she stands out. The other is how much millions of people love her. Ellen Degeneres may prefer jeans and minimalist makeup, but that hasn't stopped her from becoming one of the most respected people in hollywood.

Succeeding as a woman in Hollywood without wearing high heels and revealing outfits is no easy task. But pretending to be a girly-girl just wasn't of interest to Ellen. Instead, she played to her strengths. Her goofy, earnest, and curious nature makes her welcoming and likable to guests and viewers alike. This formula pays in spades. Her talk show has won 32 Emmys since 2003!

In the right place, being a tomboy may be a huge blessing. For instance, it will allow you to be taken seriously in certain fields that are dominated by men. In a lot of situations, however, your tomboy ways are going to get you strange looks. But that's okay. You are much better off being a comfortable, approachable tomboy than a stiff, awkward imitation of whoever might be stylish at the moment. Just look at how well it worked for Ellen!

8) Am I TOO sexy because I am...BLONDE

When Jessica Simpson burst into the scene, people  went gaga for her dream-girl-next-door look. But soon her fame turned into infamy as some of her not-so-smart comments made her the butt of a steady stream of jokes about blondes.

No need to shed tears for this starlet, though. Jessica knows her strengths and plays by them. Her good looks and positive attitude have allowed her to succeed in showbiz as both a singer and an actress. She's no brainiac, but she knows how to work with what she's got and maximize her potential. And she does it with a smile - keeping an upbeat attitude about who she is and what she's been given.

We all have our strengths and our faults. There is no need to be perfect—it's exhausting and self-defeating to try. But regardless of what life has given you—you will find that you go much farther with a good attitude and a clever approach.

9) Am I TOO sexy because I am...SARCASTIC

This man's quotes always make me snort with laughter. If you are the tongue-in-cheek, sarcastic type, you already know who this is; Groucho Marx—an extremely witty comedian and actor.

Groucho was not your ordinary warm, pleasant, smiley-faced actor; he had a cutting sense of humor which appealed to those with an appreciation for an edgier, yet funny dose of reality. He never cared much for what people thought of him, and maintained his odd signature look —horn-rimmed glasses, thick eyebrows and an even thicker mustache—throughout his career. Groucho's wit made him famous in his heyday, and largely why he's remembered.

Being too acidic won't win friends, but if there's an unpopular truth to be told, keep in mind that a spoonful of sugar (laughter!) makes the medicine go down. Groucho is just one of a myriad of people who are able to make money by packaging their soap boxes with a smile.

Today, folks like Jon Stewart and Stephen Colbert have become popular, rich and influential by speaking truth to power—in a way that makes their fans crack up. You, too, can learn to use that natural sarcastic streak to draw attention to problems and yet appear friendly and approachable. Who knows—you might even figure out how to laugh all the way to the bank.

Dealing with the anti-TOO's: A sense of humor goes a long way...

Now that you realize many famous people from both the past and present had a TOO factor, I hope that you get the message that it is okay to be different; in fact, it's better than okay, it's a blessing! If only the rest of the world realized that, right? Embracing your TOO factor stops other people from taunting you about it. How can you gracefully deal with the people who mock and taunt you? These are your options:

A. Ignore them, pretend they don't exist
B. Throw dirt in their faces
C. Laugh it off
D. Smile but secretly cry about it

At some point or another, you may have tried—or at least felt like trying—all those answers. But the best choice is always to LAUGH IT OFF! There's a reason people say "laughter is the best medicine." It's easy to think that things—particularly things about yourself—are a big deal, but if you take yourself too seriously, your life is bound to be dark and miserable. Remember from the poll, CONFIDENCE is the number one sexiness factor. All confident people are comfortable enough to joke about themselves—without feeling twisted up about it on the inside.

If people who taunt you see that you can make jokes about yourself, you will take the fun of taunting away from them. Once they see it does not affect you, they will stop taunting you altogether...especially when they know you always have a comeback that will leave them red-faced! And your ability to use humor and show self-assurance will only increase your sexiness. By embracing yourself and your "flaws" enough to laugh at them, you have effectively kept the power for yourself that the naysayers were stealing from you. See now how a little wit and humor can go a long way?

Here are just a few quips you can use to deflect taunts coming your way:

If you're taunted for being too geeky...
- When you are working for me, remember I like my coffee white, two sugars.
- If I weren't a geek, who would develop the cure for cancer?
- I'm just giving everyone else's brains a break

If you're taunted for being too big ...
- My inner child just takes up a lot of space.
- I can survive a severe famine; can you?
- This is my way of helping to stop the economic crisis; I keep fast food chains in business.

If you're taunted for being too short...
- When I lock myself out of the house, I get to use the doggy door.
- When I run out of laundry, I can just borrow my kid's clothes.
- That's how I know who keeps farting around here.

If you're taunted for being too tall...
- I guess I'm the only one who knows what fresh air smells like.
- I never get lost in crowds.
- I can reach even the highest shelf.

I'm sure you get the drift by now. Moral of the story? Make light of the situation and always have a come-back. Remember, the point of using humor is not to turn the tables on people and make them feel bad. You don't want to be part of the cycle of hurt.

But what if you're thinking "I'm just not funny", or "I freeze when I'm on the spot." Like any skill, humor is something that you can learn and improve on. Just fake it until it comes natural. In fact, take time right now to write down a few quips that could come in handy when the Anti-TOO's come for you! Google jokes about your TOO factor for inspiration, if you have to.

Chapter Review: Revealing truths that you never knew were in you

- Being different does not mean I'm not cool and sexy
- Actually, what makes me different is what makes me sexy-TOO sexy!
- Almost everybody who is somebody in this world was once labeled a misfit, and proved that their TOO factor made them sexy... and much more.
- If I can remain confident and humorous about my TOO factor, eventually no one will bother me about it

2. THE MAKING OF STEREOTYPES

Have you ever wondered who decides what's sexy and what's not? Honestly, I had never given it much thought until I started brainstorming this book. Where did I get my ideas on what I should and shouldn't do in order to fit in well in society? Before reading on, I encourage you to think of and write down at least three things that influence your actions in trying to be "cool and sexy." Again, from the unscientific poll, these were the top 4 determinants of what's hot and what's not:

1. Celebrities: they have the looks and bodies we aspire to and set the pace of what's in and what's out in terms of style and fashion.

2. The Music Industry: from music lyrics and videos I can tell what I should care about, how I should act, and how I should dress and move.

3. Style sections in the media: from TV segments to style and fashion magazines, we are spoon-fed the latest looks

4. Reality TV and TV shows: shows that revolve around sexy and successful people show me what it takes to be considered sexy.

So I got thinking, what do all these influencers have in common? They are all things we perceive through the media. Think about it: every TV show you see, every magazine you flip through, every music video you watch, every song you listen to, every commercial you sit through is telling—no, telling is not the word—is commanding you on how to think, look and dress so as to be considered an desirable member of society. How many times have you looked at someone in the media and thought if you could look like them, you'd be all set? And just like that, you already believe that you are not sexy enough.

Ironically, the people who are so influential in how we feel about ourselves and what we think we're supposed to look like are a product of the media themselves. Celebrities have to play the game along with everyone else—in fact, their livelihood depends on it. As long as they think, look, and dress right, they can be famous for anything, no matter how non-important. (The Kardashians are a great case in point!) And even more ironically, who gives people like the Kardashians the power to be so successful? The people who tune in every week and snatch up the supermarket tabloids. Us! The same people who think they are not sexy enough because of the very media we are supporting.

The more I thought about it, the more I realized I was missing something from the equation. What do the media have to gain by making sure people think, act, feel, look and dress a certain way? For them it doesn't matter if you're Hispanic, Caucasian, tall, short, big, small, old, young....all that matters is that you stay tuned to their channel. And why do they want you to stay tuned? So that they can have high viewership or listenership or readership ratings.

That was my light bulb moment: the media wants high ratings so that they can attract sponsorships and advertising dollars, which come from corporations. And how do the corporations make their money? By creating a market for your "needs"—needs they and the media create. In other words, YOUR INSECURITIES ARE THE CASH COWS OF THE CORPORATE ENTITIES.

Let me explain. The intelligent corporate fat cats know that a world full of confident people would not translate into profits. Remember how sexy confidence is? Confident people are comfortable with both their inner and outer being. They are not easily stirred to doubt themselves and are rarely plagued with insecurities.

Let's take the case of my friend Renee. Renee is a sporty twenty eight-year old. She is an assistant editor at a well-known magazine. Renee has always had a small frame, and not surprisingly, this package comes with a small bust. Her place of work exposes her to all types of beautiful women, some very curvy, others very buxom... it's a land of beautiful women. Several of her colleagues and friends keep pestering her to "fill out all that emptiness up there".

Fortunately, Renee is blessed with uber-confidence. Despite being surrounded by well-endowed women, she remains comfortable with who she is as a person. She knows that boob jobs do not equate to beauty and happiness. She has no desire to enlarge her breasts to feel good about herself—she already feels good about herself exactly as she is!

In a world full of Renees, how would the consumer corporations survive? By consumer corporation I am mostly referring to companies in these industries: cosmetics surgery, weight-loss, beauty, alcohol and fashion. Each alone rakes in billions of dollars each year—all on the backs of our insecurities. Yet there would be little to no need for their products if people were comfortable with themselves just the way they are; if they had self-acceptance.

What is the best way companies have of making sure their sales grow year after year and maintain high profitability? Easy! Shatter people's confidence by creating such high levels of insecurities that people will cling to their products to give them confidence; the confidence that they have been brainwashed into believing they do not have and can only get from their products. It's an alarmingly simple process:

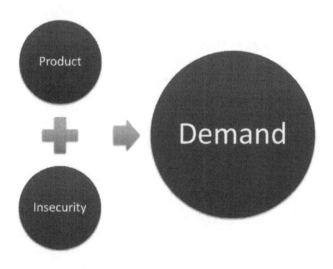

And the bigger the demand, the better the profits. So company X creates a product, then puts out commercials and other marketing material to create insecurity in a certain area of your life. By doing so, the company persuades you into thinking that without product Y, you can't be truly happy—so you go ahead and buy product Y. The result? Profitability for company X.

Nothing wrong with that... except what do you get out of it? At the end of the day, do you feel like a better, stronger, smarter, more sexy you? If the answer is ever no—and it almost always is, then this cycle of insecurity and buying is not doing you any favors.

Go to the next page to check out a table I drew up with some of the most common insecurities companies push on us. Note that almost all these product point out that you are either TOO much of something or not enough of it!

Product	Selling Point	Implied Message
Body-Building Supplements	Promises a firm, muscular, and irresistible body.	Girls like muscles. Your body is just not manly enough.
Breast Enlargement	Stop missing out on the hotties. Say hello to a new level or hotness.	Your bust is too small. You can't possibly be attractive.

Weight Loss (pills, surgery etc)	No need to exercise when a pill can make you skinny.	You're too large. You cannot be fat and sexy at the same time.
Beauty (plastic surgery)	There's no need to put up with your flaws. Get the dream look you want.	Your look is far from perfect. Fix your faults so you can be sexy.
Beauty (makeup)	Now you can achieve society's view of beauty.	Your face is flawed and plain. You have to hide to be attractive.
Male Organ Enhancement	Don't be fooled. Size DOES matter. A lot.	You're not big enough to please your woman.
Performance Enhancers (Brain)	This will help you ace your exam or your interview.	Your brain is not up to the job; you need all the help you can get.
Alcohol	Get drunk to have fun and seem desirable.	You're not cool unless you get wasted.

I'm sure you recognize the trend. Insecure people are gullible, even desperate. They can easily be swayed to do anything. This insecurity then becomes the beginning of something I call "The Hamster Wheel Projects."

No matter how fast or long a hamster runs, it will end up in the same place it started out in. This is just fine for an actual hamster, who has calories to burn and nowhere to go. But when a human takes on a hamster project—burning time, money, and emotional energy—it is nothing short of tragic. Yet most Americans spend a great deal of their lives running around in circles. I dissect the most common Hamster Wheel Projects below. Which ones leave you spinning your wheels?

Hamster Wheel Project 1: Weight-Loss Obsession

I remember a time when women were proud of their curves and maintained a healthy weight. Now, I still can't believe there is such a thing as a size 0. We live in a time when models actually die of self-induced starvation in their obsessive pursuit of "beauty." A time when self-created diseases such as bulimia and anorexia are on the rise among our youth (and are exported to developing countries alongside access to television). A time when you it's nearly impossible to be in the entertainment industry unless you have the "acceptable" weight.

What has this pursuit of the "perfect body" brought us? A nation of strong, healthy individuals? Just the opposite! A nation of insecure women uncomfortable with their weight. When did this obsession begin? When did it become a crime to not fit into a size 8 pair of jeans?!

I'll tell you how I think it began. Once again, the corporate fat cats were swirling around their chairs, wondering what next venture would lead to killer profits.

"Aha! I got it!" said one of them. "The human body naturally stores fat in select areas as an energy reservoir for emergency situations. It would make no sense to sell people products that enhance this energy-storing capacity because their body naturally does this, and so our products wouldn't sell. What if we go the opposite way? We can make fat look like the enemy and make the world believe that the less you weigh, the healthier you will be and the more attractive you will become. Then we can create weight-loss products and they shall sell like hot-cakes." And claps went round the boardroom; the first hamster wheel project had been conceived.

Ironically, the hot-cakes industry won out, too, as to many people who found they couldn't fit unrealistic standards went the other way, and comforted themselves with calorie-rich, nutrient-poor foods. Today, weight loss is a multi-billion dollar industry -- and we're less healthy than ever. It's hard to name people who haven't gotten on this hamster wheel at least once -- and most of us do it again and again. And who are the winners here? Not you or I.

As a disclaimer, I do understand that one needs to eat right and exercise right, and that habits like overeating and a sedentary lifestyle are harmful to one's health. Being overweight to the point it impacts your mobility is by no means healthy. It needs to be treated by eating the right foods in the right proportions and exercising regularly.

What I'm talking about here is the unexplainable obsession in today's world to weigh next to nothing! Do you know how futile that is? If you starve your body by eating less than you need to, it will assume it's in starvation mode. As a result, when you do eat, your body will carefully store those few calories because it assumes it doesn't know when its next supply of food will come from. Worse, calorie-deprived bodies scream out that they need more than they're getting and, more often than not, this leads to binging to satisfy those monster cravings. The binging leads to guilt, the guilt to more over-eating and harsh self-criticism, and the cycle begins anew, perhaps with an even more drastic diet than before.

Most of the weight-loss pills are actually appetite suppressants—and do little to nothing to burn the fat your body already has. Once you get off the pills, your appetite comes flooding back and more often than not, you will gain more than what you lost. Sadly, going back to taking the pills constantly may have irreversible side-effects on your body.

What is my point? All these miraculous weight loss inventions go against the natural working of the body systems and consequently are not sustainable. I know that, you may also know that, and the companies that make them sure as heck know that. But you are kept hooked to every new weight-loss invention because of your insecurity about your weight. If you can dance with your partner or your child for as long as you feel like it, if you can get through all the daily activities you want to do without feeling exhausted, if your doctor gives you a clean bill of health, that means your weight is not compromising your health and you are already at a good weight. No one should tell you otherwise. Just because you do not have a figure like Beyonce does not mean you are not sexy. There is probably something about you that Beyonce herself doesn't have and would envy you about!

Hamster Wheel Project 2: Anti-Ageing

Ah yes, another great project from Fat Cats Incorporated. If there's one thing in life that's certain (other than death and taxes) it's that we'll all grow old. Aging is a natural process and except for the tragic instances when people die young, everybody will eventually age... The Curious Case of Benjamin Button aside!

In Africa, the most revered people in society are the elderly. Why? Because they have the most experience and thus the most wisdom. They're valuable members of society and their opinions are highly respected. Africa aside, what does the rest of the world associate aging with? A lot of negative ideas: death, dependency, sagging skin, and health problems.

But old age is not as terrible as it is made out to be. I know a lot of couples in their 50's and above who are actually beginning to enjoy their lives in their old age: They are at the peak of their careers and fewer financial pressures and their children have moved out. Once retirement hits, they have more time to travel together, more time to volunteer in ways they find meaningful, and more time to pursue all those hobbies and interests they had set aside in their pursuit of the rat race. For people who have worked hard all their lives, retirement is a time to relax and enjoy what life has to offer.

But what have the fat cats done with this? They have turned old age into something to be frightened of as opposed as something to look forward to. And they have created a massive industry surrounding products to keep you from looking old. Another hamster wheel affair; no matter how much anti-aging this and anti-aging that you put on, the fact remains that your age won't change. No amount of Botox and cosmetic surgery can change that fact. The best way to keep young at heart despite your age is to surround yourself by the things and people that make you happy. Eating right and exercising help too, of course. And don't obsess about what you're like on the outside, while ignoring what that's doing to your mind and soul.

Instead of buying a houseful of products and undergoing expensive surgical procedures all in the hope of reviving your youthful looks, accept that your youth is behind you. Embrace the good things that being older has to offer. Despite what you see or hear from the media and from commercials, permanent youth is unattainable. You are young for a reason. Make the most of your youth so that when you're older, you're not trying to relive it. Instead, look at your older self as a wiser you and enjoy this phase of your new journey.

A friend of mine always talks about how her family makes her look forward to aging. They have tackled so many wonderful new activities in their 50s and 60s. It's as if they are experiencing their own Renaissance. Their confidence shines through and makes them wanted assets in their communities. However, if you're always worrying about how old you look, you will never be confident about yourself, and you can't be sexy without confidence—no matter how wrinkle-free your face might be.

Does this mean you shouldn't take interest and pride in how you look? Of course not. Put on that smart jacket, try that new 'do. Take care of your skin by not smoking or exposing yourself to too much UV light. But don't obsess over every new age spot or wrinkle—those things you have earned; wear them with pride.

We've all seen older ladies and gentlemen who have an air about them. These people demand to be noticed—their posture, smiles, and way they put themselves together just draw us in. We notice their debonair bearing or ageless grace not because of the amount of work they've had done to themselves, but because of ... yes, there it is again... their TOO sexy level of confidence. Emulate those people and you will go far.

The next time you see some ad claiming its product is the guaranteed path to the fountain of youth, remember two things:

· Just like the fountain of youth, the age-defying product is an urban myth!

· No need for you to slather on anti-aging creams and undergo Botox; you're TOO sexy just the way you are!

Hamster Wheel Project 3: Body Image

Beauty, as the saying goes, is in the eyes of the beholder. In other words, beauty is relative. What one person considers beautiful is not necessarily what another person considers beautiful. One way to think about this is that you can't possibly hope to please everyone; on the other hand, we are all beautiful in one respect or another. And we can all be beautiful, confident people.

However, once again the Overlords have discovered that if people think they possess good looks, they will not have an incessant need to purchase a myriad of products to beautify themselves. No insecurities equals no profits. Thus, they created the ideal man and woman for us mere mortals to forever strive for.

We all know how the ideal woman should look:
- flawless skin: acne-free, hair-free and an even skin tone
- slim waist (preferably a size zero)
- skinny, fat-free body but still curvy
- long hair
- perfect pearly whites
- full lips

Men have not been spared, either:
- Tall
- Six-pack
- Broad shoulders
- Chiseled jaw
- Defined body
- Full hair

How many people fit these ideals?

A lot of pressure has been purposely created to cleverly coerce people to be insecure about themselves should they dare to deviate from this image. Unfortunately, since achieving this body image ideal is as likely as attaining world peace, deviate they will. I mean, what is the likelihood of having a body free of so-called "faults"? Two great myths have been fed to you to create massive insecurity about your body image:

1)I can look like that if I work hard enough

This lie is bigger than the Grand Canyon, and is intended to incentivize you to purchase products you don't need. The ideal woman was created to ensure that all women work towards achieving this all-but-unattainable goal. To get women thinking "if I just buy that skin firming cream, I can say goodbye to cellulite." Or "if I could just use this electric slimming belt, I will be tummy-free." But it's not just the cellulite or the tummy—not that these products work to begin with. It's hair color, length, and style; eye, cheek, lip, and chin color; nail shape and color; shape and size of cleavage; and the list goes on and on. Men face a similar dilemma—that protein powder and that exercise machine coupled with that shampoo and that aftershave are just the start of what's needed.

The clever overlords know it's impossible to obtain all the qualities of the so-called ideals—that's the whole point. It forces people to spend tons of money trying to get this image, running around like, you guessed it, a hamster in its wheel. Insecurities for you equal profits for them. This is the wool that has been pulled over your eyes! The only women alive who can come close to the ideal image were born with an amazing, improbable set of genetics, and then augmented them through obsessive diet and exercise, and very expensive and numerous skin-care products, topped off by "corrective" surgery. And photoshop.

If that sounds exhausting, that's because it is. The most "desirable" people in the world are just as insecure than the rest of us, if not more so, because they know exactly how much it takes to get close to that ideal... and because they feel the brunt of not meeting the ideal every time they gain a few pounds or are seen in public without their full hair-and-makeup regimen.

As a side note, I despise the term "corrective". It suggests there was something wrong in the first place. The only thing that's wrong - and it's a big one -- is that you have been robbed of your confidence and do not even realize it! Striving to meet the ideal image makes no economic sense. Why spend almost all the money you make trying to get social acceptance by paying for an unsustainable, unattainable ideal image? I say unsustainable because—as the stars themselves show, one Botox treatment or facelift or tummy tuck isn't enough. People who strive to be perfect have to go under the knife again and again because... People. Aren't. Perfect.

Isn't it easier (and cheaper) to develop a sense of confidence and accept yourself as you are? Look at the hundred richest people in the world. Do they try to adhere to these standards? These are savvy, hardworking people—so smart they have managed to make it the world's top 100 richest people. These people are brilliant enough to be phenomenally wealthy, and they have more than enough money to pay for the ideal body image, yet they opt to stay as they are. Doesn't that tell you that they are smart enough to realize that they don't need to adhere to a commanded body image to be confident about themselves and their capabilities? Their confidence in who they are and not what they look like is a major contributing factor to how far they have gotten in life.

If you are going to imitate someone, why follow the celebrities who are stuck in the same hamster wheel you are? Be like the people who know that actions speak louder than looks. And if your friends and partner will only accept you if you torture yourself in an attempt to reach this ideal image, you need a new set of friends!

2) The people I see on the media have the perfect face & body: Beautiful People Fallacy

I find it interesting how we often take what we see on the media at face value and as gospel truth. Every minute or so, a beauty-related advertisement appears on TV--a hot blonde gets every man she wants, or a rock-star guy has to fend the ladies off all because of 'secret'(the advertised beauty product) revealed at the end of the ad. What this is sublimely telling the viewer is that you cannot be attractive unless you look like the people on the screen. Another ad appears...now this one shows a sculpted man attracting all the ladies in the room or a toned, yet curvy woman. Like the other ad, the 'secret' to the sexual attractiveness is not diligent exercise and a common-sense diet, but some product promising you muscle gain in seconds. (Okay, I've exaggerated a little-- muscle gain in minutes.)

It's easy to be skeptical about any one given commercial or ad. Our problem is that we are pummeled by an onslaught of images of unachievable beauty—on TV, in glossy magazines, on billboards. It's hard—if not impossible—to resist the message when it's drilled so thoroughly into us throughout our entire lives.

Yet it's important to resist these messages. The ideal image you are trying to reach is not even real! All these images of "beautiful people" have been perfected in order for consumers to believe they can achieve these physical impossibilities by merely buying product X.

Let me take you behind the scenes of these adverting shoots. Believe me, a lot of creativity—not to say outright manipulation—goes into the making of these ads. It starts with professional make-up and hairdressing, then moves on to clever lighting and ingenious angles that enhance the right parts while downplaying the flaws. But that's hardly enough. Even with all those advantages (not to mention a heavy dose of natural beauty or handsomeness) the models and actors need to be airbrushed and Photoshopped.

In other words, by the time the advertising teams are done making a model "perfect," their own mothers would barely recognize them! Yet this is the image you try to attain and maintain every day. The people you see on these media channels do not look like their ad-selves; a lot of hard work goes into making them look like that! I encourage you to google "celebs with and without make up" photos. See for yourself why you it's a waste of time and energy to sigh whenever you see your favorite actor/actress on TV and wish to look like that!

This hamster wheel project has swept over the world, and is causing more and more women -- and, increasingly, men - to hate themselves and consequently loose the one thing that make people sexy: CONFIDENCE.

Open your eyes and realize there are powerful people in this world who don't want you to believe you are sexy just the way you are so that they can profit from your insecurities. It is up to you to stop buying the lie that you are not sexy enough as you are. This lie is too costly -- both to your pocketbook and to your self-esteem. It is time to go back to the store and return this big, fat lie and tell the salesperson, "I want my confidence back. This big fat lie doesn't look good on me."

Chapter Review: Revealing truths that you never knew were in you:

- My insecurities are continuously created and rejuvenated purely for profit at the expense of my happiness
- Not everything I see in the media is true
- If my doctor declares me healthy, my weight is A-OK!
- Perpetual youth is a myth. Ageing is a natural process. I shouldn't fight it; I should embrace it and age with grace
- If the advert models don't even look a thing like their ad-selves, then clearly the use of the advertised products will not significantly change how I look.
- I should accept myself as I am, with all my media-labeled 'flaws'. Only then will I obtain the confidence that will actually make me sexy -- TOO sexy!

3. BREAKING THE BONDS

By now you are fully aware of why you might believe you're not good enough. Years of consistent misinformation has ingrained it in you that you're not enough of this or TOO much of that to be considered sexy. From deceitful commercials, to TV shows dictating what's sexy and what's not, to magazines telling you how to achieve an unattainable and unsustainable look, to your own friends and loved ones telling you what's "wrong" about you, you've spent your life on the wrong end of a painful avalanche.

When you think about it this way, it's quite surprising that despite all these negative voices in our daily lives, we still manage to wake every morning and face the world. Yes, we can face the world—but not conquer it. We are living as mere shadows of ourselves. We have been told over and over again—even by our own internal critiques—how unsexy we are. Living this way, a good day is when you manage to not frown too deeply at the image in the mirror. A day when you can avoid attracting negative comments.

We all have the potential to be great in one way or another. But how can you achieve your own greatness if you do not have the confidence to be yourself? You are sexy just the way you are. You just need to believe it! But how do you flush out years of deceit from your system? How do you start believing in yourself again? How do you finally boost your TOO sexy levels? These nine fantastic steps are your path to a better, happier, TOO sexy you:

1) Mirror, mirror on the wall...

Tell yourself five things you love about you every day. Remind yourself of them as often as you need to. Psychologists call this positive reinforcement. Insecurities don't exist in the real world. They're tricks of the mind that cause you to believe you're not enough of something or too much of something else. If you're like most people, you greet your reflection every morning with a frown as you look at your "flaws."

Since the mirror cannot actually talk to you and tell you all the good things you are, do it for yourself. Think of five things you love about yourself. They could be physical characteristics (your chocolate eyes, your strong shoulders or your ready smile), personality traits (your loyalty, your curiosity, or your kindness), or even things you've gotten right in your life (you're a good parent or sibling; you impress people at work). The five things could be a combination of traits you secretly love about yourself and that other people compliment you on. It doesn't matter, as long as you write five solid things, with no "buts" attached to them.

Hopefully, you'll have no problem coming up with five things—or even more. But if you have spent too much time in a toxic environment, you might find yourself struggling. This is NOT because you lack wonderful traits, but because you have become too harsh a critique. If you are struggling to come up with five things, don't skimp. Just reach until you find something, no matter how small. Maybe your finger-nails are in good shape; maybe people always compliment you on your contribution to the potluck. Start small and as you go through your daily affirmations and the rest of your steps, you will find it easier to think of bigger and better things to say about yourself.

Once you've nailed down your five things, write them in big letters on a sticky note and paste them on your mirror. That way, every time you glance at the mirror, you can remember that while you may not have lips like Angelina Jolie, you have thick, flowing hair to die for!

Don't expect sticky note affirmation to work overnight! You have a lifetime of negative messages to overcome. It will take approximately one month for those five things to sink in. Keep your notes up for one month. By the time the month is over, no one will be able to shake your confidence in your sexiness of those five things. The next month, come up with five new things to love about yourself.

Start a new list every month, and in exactly one year's time, you'll be able to confidently state 60 things that make you sexy. That might seem like an impossible amount, even if you feel pretty self-assured to begin with, but it's not. You'll see. There are 60 fantastic things about you—is that TOO sexy, or what!

2) Beauty is...

Keep a journal or personal blog where you write out your reflections on your own beauty. Beauty itself is largely misconstrued to be all about how you look physically. Truthfully, beauty is not just about how we appear. Beauty can be the way in which you do things, the way in which you conduct yourself, and the way in which you treat others. Rather than summing up the total beauty you possess as what you look like on the outside, view your beauty as all the things that you are and you do which are worthwhile.

You already do truly beautiful things, even without giving yourself credit for them. Writing these things down forces you to acknowledge them (yes—you may need to give yourself permission to admit you are beautiful; that is how twisted our culture has made us). Reading back your notes will remind you how beautiful you are day in and day out. Even when you don't conform to the created perception of beauty. The beautiful way you act is what makes you unique and lovable.

Writing down what makes you beautiful acts as a constant reminder that no matter what you perceive from the media, you too are beautiful, and people appreciate a lot of beautiful things about you. Another advantage of keeping a journal of such information is that you will be able to see your daily growth—from an insecure person to a confident, sexy person nobody can bring down.

Doing something new challenges your comfort level, and starting a beauty journal is no different. If you are feeling intimidated by all those blank pages, or feel silly about writing down certain thoughts or feelings, don't worry—it's only natural. But you have to do it anyway (Yes, guys, too. Call it "attractiveness" if it makes you feel better.) Here are some ideas to get you started:

Beauty is...

- sharing a whole-hearted smile with a loved one.
- leaving the house without make-up on, and still having the confidence to flirt with someone who catches your eye.
- holding your head high, even in the most undig-nifying situations.
- being able to leave a no-good partner, knowing that you deserve and will get better.
- dancing in public to a song you love, without fear of judgment.
- being proud of your history and heritage and making no apologies for where you come from.
- laughing freely and spontaneously, without try-ing too hard to appear cool.
- Loving someone who loves you back exactly as you are and wouldn't change you for the world.

By now you get the drift. Beauty doesn't have to be tied down to the size of your waist or the length of your legs. Beauty is how you live your everyday life. Give yourself credit for what really counts, even though the corporate fat cats don't try to package it! Give yourself credit for the TOO Sexy already in you!

3) Exercise, Eat Right

When your body is in tiptop shape, it releases feel-good hormones, improves your mood, and boosts your energy levels—not to mention betters your health! All the benefits of regular exercise make it easier to love yourself and increase your self-confidence. Combine this with eating foods that are good for you and have no negative side effects, you'll feel on top of the world!

You won't believe all the great reasons to exercise and eat right:

The TOO Sexy's benefits of healthy living:
- Better health, fewer illnesses
- Improved mood
- Reduced stress and cope better
- Increased self-esteem
- Increased energy levels
- Improved libido and sexual enjoyment
- The death of depression
- Improved mental performance
- Permanent Weight loss
- Better, more restful sleep
- Clearer skin
- Less visible cellulite
- Aging gracefully
- Milder PMS

People assume healthy living is the end of culinary enjoyment. That it's all about dieting and killing yourself at the gym. This isn't true at all! Living healthy simply means eating enough of the right foods, limiting the intake of harmful foods, and keeping your body active through exercise to avoid excess storage of fat. For instance, junk food is a nutrient-starved option that makes you pile on the pounds without even giving you the proper nutrition your body needs, hence the craving for more.

You don't have to eat bland foods and die of exhaustion at the gym to live healthy. In fact, overexerting yourself can be as harmful as not getting enough exercise. And whole shelves of cookbooks with delicious, healthy foods are waiting for you to enjoy. In fact, research shows that you can have a wide variety of foods to maintain a healthy lifestyle. I would advise everyone reading this book to consult with a nutritionist on meal choices they can follow that are rich in nutrients, healthy, and still delicious. Unlike crazy dieting, eating healthy is sustainable because you can eat the right foods without feeling starved or being tempted to binge.

Exercise does not have to be about willing yourself to knowingly punish your body excessively. You can partake in several different activities to remain healthy and active. Most are hobbies and you can still have fun while shedding the extra pounds and keeping fit. For instance, some people find that jogging or running puts them in the "zone," whereas others would prefer to zumba their cares away or my personal favorite SALSA dance my cares away. You are free to pick what you feel works best for you. Just pick your fave activity and—here's the crucial part—make it a habit. It all adds up to a new, TOO sexy you!

On the next page, you'll find a brief list of sports and activities you can take up. The number of calories you will burn depends on a variety of factors, such as your weight, your exercise intensity, and your metabolism. This list will give you an idea of the relative amount of calories lost, though. Even calmer activities like bicycling for fun, strolling around the park, doing yoga and even cleaning the house can add up, especially if you do them for long enough each day.

Activity	Calories lost per half-hour
Running	450
Rock Climbing	371
Swimming	360
Cycling	350
Boxing	324
Racquetball	300
Basketball	288

4) Amputate

I'm not talking about chopping your leg off! However, we can learn something from the reasoning behind amputation. Removing an infected or damaged part of the body saves the rest of you from infection and consequently spares your life. Amputation is no small thing, requiring people to decide to let go of one part of their body so as to save the rest. Though a painful process—both physically and emotionally—it is not just an obvious choice, but a necessary one.

The same applies to social amputation. Everybody—and I mean everybody—has had at least one friend, family member, or significant other who always gets them down. This person is the constant negative voice in your head, telling you you're simply not good enough. Every time you inject some positivity into the conversation, this person quickly shoots you down and tells you a million reasons why your idea is bad and will never work out.

This is the same type of person who would discourage you from buying this book—if you had the guts enough to mention it in front of them. This person literally stops you from growing to become a better you. Deadweight, to put it frankly.

Why even hang out with Mr. or Mrs. Negativity? The typical response is: "We've been friends for so long" or "We've dated for so long." But this is truly a misguided and damaging sense of loyalty. If there's a toxic person in your life right now, you need to stop and ask yourself what value this person is adding to your life.

If you have fast-spreading breast cancer, it would be better to have your breast removed than to allow the cancer to spread over your whole body. In the same way, it is better to detach yourself from negative friends who always pull you down instead of lift you up. It sounds harsh, but it's true. You are putting more caring and concern into the relationship than the other person merits. And it's important that you get rid of their poisonous influence. It is nearly impossible to believe you are sexy when "friends" are seemingly trying their best to make you feel anything but.

Why do people act this way in the first place? These folks also have issues with their image—usually more so than the average person, no matter how well-put-together they might look on the outside. They don't know how to handle the issues themselves, so they pass them off to you. No matter how cruel their inner voice is, they can be comforted by the fact that the people around them are even sadder than they are. Nice, right? And that's the kind of friendship you're worried about ditching?

Don't let someone else weigh you down or make you doubt your self-worth. Just leave that toxic friendship behind. True, dumping a friend or lover is not easy. Try thinking of yourself as the body that needs to be saved from the deadly cancer.

In case your stomach gets tied in knots just at the thought of cutting the... ehem... knot, here are a few useful tips on how to detach yourself from negative friends or lovers:

- Reduce communication. Stop calling and texting them. Let them be the ones to make the first move—every single time. Eventually they will notice the relationship has become a one-way street. Because they won't stand for an insult to their self-esteem, they will stop communicating.

- If you're bold enough, confront them and tell them you sincerely dislike the fact that all they do is make you feel bad about yourself. Tell them that if they cannot change, you will call it quits. An ultimatum will let them know how serious you are about the need for an attitude change.

- Seek therapy. This person is your friend for a reason—birds of a feather flock together. If your friend is negative, there's a good chance you play into that cycle somehow. Maybe you play victim to their aggressor, or maybe you're both catty about other people, and you just don't enjoy it when the tables are turned on you. Suggest seeking professional help together. That way you can both tackle the root cause of your negativity. Plus, you can still remain friends who help build each other up, instead of bringing each other down.

Deciding to completely leave a person is tough. But giving them a chance to change for the better together is like having chemotherapy or radiation treatment. It's a long process with lots of side effects and the potential to not work. Giving people the benefit of the doubt is very generous, but it can be harmful. You can't force anyone to change, so you have to be strong enough to realize when the "treatment" is not working. Remember, without that daily presence breathing self-doubt and low self-esteem into your life, your confidence levels will soar. And as you well know, there's nothing sexier than that!

5) Re-group

As the saying goes, out with the old, in with the new. Alcoholics in A.A know they must avoid friends and environments that would lead them down that road again. But they also know the importance of filling that vacuum. Once you've successfully ridden yourself of negative friends, your next step is to make positive friends who will build you up and help you develop a sense of confidence. But how do you go about this?

First, not all your friends tear you down; once you've weeded out the negative ones, invite the positive ones to a gathering. You could plan a night out, a day at the spa or the sports stadium, even a sleepover....whatever your choice. The point is to reconnect with these upbeat, uplifting friends. The thoughts and feelings of positive friends are just as contagious as those of negative folks, except this is the kind of contagion you want.

Research has actually proven that people who surround themselves with happy and encouraging people are usually much happier than those who don't. So pick up the phone and invite your sunshiny friends to a fun-filled get-together.

Second, now is a good time to expand your social network. Meet new people who are also going through the same process you are; people who want to change their lives for the better by getting rid of their insecurities and gaining back their confidence. Attend events where you're likely to meet such people: talks by motivational speakers who emphasize building up self-esteem, book clubs that focus on self-help books, or even anonymous groups for people dealing with insecurities. Reaching out to others in the same boat will show you that you are not the only one who is struggling with insecurities. Furthermore, you and your new friends can encourage each other to fulfill your mutual goals -- to work on your insecurities and become TOO sexy.

6) Your TOO sexy mentor

Success is 10% inspiration and 90% perspiration. That means anything worth doing is worth working on, hard. That's what the other parts of this book are about -- putting in that 90% to get to a confident, TOO sexy you. But what about the 10%?

Everybody could use some inspiration when working to achieve a difficult goal. This is where a mentor comes in handy. Think about all the people in your life -- whether they be close friends or distant acquaintances. Then ask yourself these questions to identify the best

TOO sexy mentor for you:

- · Is this a confident person who I admire?
- · Has this person overcome any barriers to become what they were today?
- · Were those barriers similar to ones I face? Or can I relate to them in some way?

- Can I trust this person with my secrets and insecurities? Will this person keep what we discuss private?
- Is this person willing to spend some time with me every so often to mentor me and keep me inspired? (Don't assume that just because you're not too close to a person, they wouldn't be interested in mentoring you. One of the privileges of being successful is helping other rise. However, you do need to be considerate of their time.)

If you find someone who meets all five requirements, excellent! You have just found yourself a guiding force on your TOO sexy journey.

One benefit of having a live mentor is that this person may introduce you to like-minded people who have also overcome the same challenge. If one mentor is good, having an entire group as a resource is even better. Hanging around powerful, positive people can do wonders to your self-esteem. It also helps you to realize that you too can become just like them by dealing with your insecurities and getting the confidence to be happy just the way you are.

Don't despair if you do not have someone in your life who can mentor you. Ask your friends if they can think of someone who can help. Chances are, somebody knows somebody! But don't stand still waiting for the right match. You can always look for inspiration from TOO sexy people in the public eye.

Chapter One of this book highlights some celebrities who overcame stereotypical challenges to get to where they are today. Use one of them as your example, or find a pioneer in your field whom you can relate to. Read about them. Record quotes that are relevant to your situation. Allow yourself to be inspired in your journey to become TOO sexy.

7) Eliminate Advertitis

Let's start by defining this addition to the dictionary. Advertitis is a highly dangerous disease of the mind. The more advertisements you watch, the more direct and subliminal messages you receive and believe regarding how unsexy you are and how insecure you ought to be about your body image. Advertitis is often characterized by low self-esteem, a lack of confidence, self-hatred, and self-blame. It leads to a willingness to spend huge sums of money on products and procedures that people in their right mind would not normally purchase.

Now that you understand the meaning of Advertitis, do you recognize yourself as suffering from it? From all those times you have looked with envy at all the beautiful people in billboards, glossy magazines and TV ads, wishing in vain that you could look like that as well?

You know from the previous chapter that it is impossible to resemble a model who only appears like that due to a lot of cosmetic work, air brushing and graphic alteration. Why continue to judge yourself against people who don't even look like their real selves? That only leads to feelings of inadequacy. My solution may seem harsh, but it is effective: stop watching advertisements altogether and to limit the time you spend watching TV.

Ask yourself, do the programs you watch really add any value to your life? So many reality TV shows, daytime soaps, and steamy prime-time dramas these days all seem to say the same thing: If you are not "hot" with bucket loads of cash, your life means nothing.

Television spoon-feeds us glamour that's not even real. How does watching shows about such people who are famous for no apparent reason improve your life? I often believe too many people waste too much time in front of their television screen. Do you waste valuable time in front of a television screen? If the answer is yes, ask yourself how exactly that may be shaping your thoughts and feeling about who you are on a daily basis. This is why the TV dictates so many people's attitudes towards themselves.

The less TV you watch, the better a person you will be. First, you will put the time that you could have wasted in front of that screen to better use. Second, you will effectively remove one of the most negative voices in your life, a voice that makes you feel close to worthless.

Give it a try. Here are is a step-by-step guide to eliminate the negative voice of TV from your life:

a. Write down all the TV shows you watch

b. Break this down into days of the week. What do you watch on Mondays, Tuesdays, Wednesdays and so forth?

c. Figure out what percent of your day (24 hours) you spend watching TV?

d. Write down what you have learned, both good and bad, from the shows you have listed.

e. Identify the shows that are not adding value to your life

f. Stop watching the non-value additional shows. It's that simple.

g. Eliminate advertisements altogether. TiVo your shows, mute the TV when the ads come up, or simply walk out of the room.

Ending a TV show addiction might not be easy, but it could be the best thing that ever happened to you. First, you will be cutting down on communication that results in insecurity and low self-esteem. Eliminating negative shows from your life will also free up your time to do things which you were too busy to do before, like exercising and hanging out with worthwhile friends. It's a win-win path to creating a TOO sexy you.

8) Theme Song Alert

Music is a powerful art that I believe connects with the soul. There' a reason practically all television shows have music to go with them. No matter how long or short, they all have a theme song which the viewer associates with the TV Show. Why not just start with the show? It would be weird, wouldn't it? The song gets you into the right mood. Supermarkets and stores play music to make you linger. Movies all use music to enhance your emotional connection and heighten your viewing experience. Suspense wouldn't be as suspenseful or love as lovely without a soundtrack paving the emotional way.

The way music works in the film industry is the same way it works for you. I have yet to meet a person who has no desire for music! Music has a magical way of reaching the soul and uplifting your spirits. This is why you need to identify a song that resonates with your resolution to be a confident, TOO sexy individual.

A personal TOO Sexy theme song will help you feel good about yourself...and what did we say about feeling good? It boosts you confidence. Keep that attitude up and you will automatically go up several notches in the sexiness table!

Playing your personal theme song in your head will also act the same way garlic does to a vampire -- it wards the haters off! Unfortunately, just because you have made up your mind to appreciate yourself exactly as you are does not mean your attitude will automatically deflect the "haters." When they cause you to doubt yourself, use your personal theme song to keep yourself focused and upbeat. Fend them off with your neat little comeback then crank up the volume on your iPod and listen to your TOO sexy jam.

What defines a truly awesome TOO sexy jam? Here are the five must-haves of a TOO sexy jam. Listening to the song and its message:

1. makes you feel special just the way you are.
2. makes you feel as confident and sexy as the person singing it.
3. makes you feel like you can conquer it all.
4. reminds you that life is not always bad; that life is beautiful.
5. is something you're happy to do over and over again!

Think of it as positive brainwashing -- if you tell yourself something over and over again, eventually you'll start believing it. Repeatedly hearing an inspirational musical number doesn't just lift your spirits. It will give you the confidence to be happy with who you are, and a confident you is definitely a TOO sexy you!

Our very insightful, unscientific poll revealed the top songs that respondents indicated would make them upbeat and determined to stay TOO sexy for life!

- "I'm too sexy" – Right Said Fred
- "I'm sexy and I know it" – LMFAO
- "Beautiful" – Christina Aguilera
- "Unpretty" – TLC
- "SexyBack"– Justin Timberlake
- "Suddenly I See" – KT Tunstell
- "Kiss" – Prince
- "Bossy" – Kelis
- "Survivor" – Destiny's Child
- "Walking on Sunshine" – Katrina & The Waves
- "I'm Every Woman" – Whitney Houston
- "Life Is Good" – LFO
- "Unwritten" – Natasha Bedingfield
- "Life Goes On" – Leann Rimes

Your TOO sexy theme song doesn't have to come from the above list; these were just the popular choices. You will know that you have found your TOO sexy jam when you hear it. When you do, make sure it stays in every musical device you own. That way, every time you need a little help reminding yourself that you are sexy, your song is right there for you.

9) One-on-None Date

Treat yourself like you deserve to be treated and take yourself on a date. I know this sounds strange, but bear with me -- it's worth it. You don't need to go somewhere fancy; on the contrary, dinner in the privacy of your home may be your best bet. That doesn't mean you can skimp on yourself; on the contrary, go all out in order to set the mood.

Splurge on a trip to the salon/barber that day and style your hair the way you like it. Once you get home, cook yourself an exquisite meal, as if you were trying to impress a date. Afterwards, take a relaxing bath and dress up for the occasion. Wear something that makes you feel hot! After you are all dressed up, serve yourself the scrumptious meal in your best dinnerware. If possible, have a candle-lit meal. Polish everything off with a good bottle of wine.

Now the date can officially begin. Talk openly about your life, what you love about it and what you love about yourself. Discuss what you can do turn the not-so-great things in your life around. Reminisce on moments in your past that made you feel at the height of your sexiness plateau. Work on figuring out what you can do to feel that sexy all the time.

By the end of the date, you will have positively reviewed your life and appreciated all the good things in it. Taking a specific, concentrated time to do this -- on a special just-for-you day -- will increase your positive attitude and confidence levels. And, you guessed it; this will create an aura of increased sexiness about you. (If your date derailed into a self-criticizing nightmare, don't despair. Check out Chapter 4 to figure out all the great things about your life and Chapter 5 to quiet your fierce inner critic.)

A date with yourself has the added benefit of preparing you for the real thing. It gives you the chance to get fully in touch with yourself and what you like about yourself -- so all those good memories and good energy can shine through when you're out with someone else.

Regardless of your dating situation, you should take time off your busy life once in a while and remind yourself why you are just TOO sexy! I guarantee this will definitely bring out the sexy in you!

Chapter Review: Revealing truths that you never knew were in you:

- Reminding myself everyday of at least five things that make me sexy will boost my confidence levels.
- Keeping a journal of things I find beautiful will help me break the stereotype of beauty fed to me by the media.
- Healthy living comes with the added benefits of im-proved self-esteem and confidence, leading to a more sexy me.
- Toxic negative friends will only hold me back. Either they change with me for the better or I leave them behind as part of my toxic past.
- I should hang out with people who are positive. They make me happy and let me to feel good about who I am just the way I am.
- Someone has already gone through and overcome what I am going through now. I need to identify this person and ask him or her to mentor me and keep me inspired.
- As part of the detox, I have to stop viewing ads and TV shows that make me feel insecure and bad about myself.

- Music is the food of the soul. A TOO Sexy theme song will keep me feeling upbeat and confident enough to feel sexy just as I am.
- Making room in my busy schedule for a solo date will give me the time remember what makes me great and boost my confidence and sexiness levels.

4. THE SEXINESS SELF-EVALUATION

A reality show in the UK, Snog Marry Avoid, features women in desperate needs of make-unders. In their misguided quest the perfect look, some of these women spend hours every day putting on layers of false eyelashes, fake hair, and makeup. Hours! Every day! Yet inevitably, people—from their friends and family to perfect strangers—prefer their stripped down, more natural look—the version without the falsies and miles of makeup. So why do these women feel like they can't leave the house with all the fakery? Because they believed the lies they were fed, and can't appreciate their true selves.

So far, you have learned why it's important to accept yourself just the way you are. You've identified the major cause of insecurities amongst the population. And you've discovered how to re-define sexiness by breaking through stereotypes.

Yet many of you are feeling far from TOO Sexy. You know what's holding you back, but you are having trouble identifying your strong points. The exercises in this chapter will help you create a huge inventory of all the ways you are fantastic. Taking stock of your traits, skills, values, and your fantastic social network will help bring out a more confident, TOO Sexy you.

Know Thyself

How would you describe yourself? You can probably come up with a few words off the top of your head, but it's important to dig deeper. For instance, a friend of mine might describe herself as smart, funny, sarcastic. But she'd be missing out on caring, loyal, and helpful.

And she'd still be selling herself short. What about all those times she's been patient even though she'd rather be doing something else? Those times she forced herself out of bed despite how much it called to her. I know she sees herself as impatient and lazy for feeling that way, but I would argue that some traits are just as important when you have to fight to have them as they are if they come naturally. Who's braver—a person who's not scared of heights, or one who is but rock climbs anyway?

In the same way, it is important that you give yourself full credit for all your wonderful personality traits. I'm sure you don't cut yourself any slack for your flaws, so it's time you do the same for your strengths.

I'm going to present you with two techniques for figuring out all the great things about you. The first you can do alone, right now. The second requires the help of friends. You can do one or the other—either will be effective in helping you on this journey. However, if you do both of them, you will be able to compare how you see yourself relative to how others see you, which can be quite enlightening.

The Solo Exercise

On the next page, I present the personality trait ball. Use it as a starting point for your own brainstorming session. Which words resonate with you? Which words seem unlike you—and yet you display them fairly often, like how you force yourself to be sociable even when you'd rather go hide.

Don't feel limited by the words in the personality ball. They are just there to get you started. In fact, I

tagxedo.com

push you to find at least five other words that describe you. Make sure you truly know why all the words you chose are on your list. Some words might come reflectively— "Of course I'm kind," but think of meaningful examples to back them up, like the time you were extra gracious to that waitress who was clearly having a bad day, even though you didn't expect to see her again. Our selves cannot be summed up in lists of words. Enrich your self-understanding by writing down concrete examples that show off your personality.

The Group Exercise

Email your friends and family individually, or use the "blind carbon copy" option. You don't want people responding to the whole group, just to you. Tell them you are working on personal development and need them to list five of your strengths.

Look through the results. See any patterns? These traits stand out to people. Any surprises? Those are areas that you might be selling yourself short. (Or, conversely, if you are surprised by what's missing from the list, maybe you are not doing a good job of letting that side of you show.)

Once again, write down concrete examples to back up the strengths on your list. If you are really stumped as to why someone said what they did, don't feel shy about emailing them back and saying "I don't see that in me. Can you tell me more?" When someone sees a light shining in you that you didn't even know was there, it's worth digging deeper.

Work Backwards

During the group exercise, did you balk at any of the descriptions your friends sent you? "How can people see me as loyal? Sure, friends are important, but that's not me." Or "Creative? Sure, I doodle a bit, but I'm hardly an artist." Instead of questioning what other people see, put yourself in their shoes. They believe what they tell you because they see evidence for it. Search for that evidence yourself. "Well, I did make chicken soup for Christine's mom when she was in the hospital," or "That presentation I made for the party was unique." Instead of selling yourself short because someone out there seems more something than you, embrace the fact that you are that something, too—and chalk it up as one more way you are TOO Sexy.

Know Your Values

Values are beliefs that affect the way you think and act. Most of us have contradicting beliefs—thus we may value both loyalty and independence, or friendship and solitude.

Some part of you must value the warped sense of attractiveness and popularity that the media sells, or you wouldn't be reading this book. But you have a plethora of other ideals to drown out the bad ones. Some stand in direct opposition to the idea of shrink-wrapped "beauty" such as honesty and purity. Other values—such as your appreciation of adventure, or stability—can be put in front of shallow desires.

Finally, you may hold values that currently fuel your negative thoughts, but could be used for your benefit. For instance, you may be using your desire for affection or pleasure in order to justify buying ridiculous beauty products. You could, however, seek pleasure in other things: good friends, fine foods, or a warm bath.

It is time you took stock of your values to see how they affect you now and where they can lead you in the future. Just follow these four steps:

    1.**Write down all your values**. You can use the image below as your starting point, but don't let it limit you. Remember, not everything you value is virtuous.

Write down all the things you find important, even the ones that would make you cringe if you had to admit them out loud.

2.**Sort your values.** Separate them into three lists: values you are proud to hold on to, misguided values you would like to change, and values that currently lead to negative thoughts and behaviors, but which could prove helpful. For the sake of this exercise, let's think of these as values you'd like to flip-flop.

3.Flesh things out. Realizing what your values are is a crucial first step, but you also need to examine how they affect your life.

- Next to each of your positive values, jot down a few notes on why it's important to you and what you can do to act on the value. For instance, you might value service because you think it's important to be a contributing member of your community, and you might act on it by taking part in Big Brothers Big Sisters now that you've cut out TV viewing time.

- Next to each flipflop value, write down how it's currently harmful and how it could be turned positive. For instance, maybe your love of aesthetics lead you to obsess over the latest fashions. But you could use it to redecorate your room so it inspires relaxation. If you realize the way you value friendships has turned you into a follower or a doormat, work on creating meaningful relationships full of mutual trust and respect.

- Next to each negative value, write down how it impacts your life. Give yourself extra credit for figuring out a way to decrease its influence. For instance, maybe your love of money makes you greedier and more selfish than you'd like to admit. If you dig deeper, you might realize you like money because having it makes you feel secure and lets you do things you enjoy— and you can achieve those goals without greed.

4.   **Rank your values.** Arrange each list separately.

- Your positive values are your arsenal. Use them to crowd out or shoot down negative thoughts and behavior. Live in a way that reflects your most important positive values, and you will find it easier to deflect the naysayers in your life.
- Your negative values are the weak spots you need to watch out for. Decrease or eliminate contact with the people, places, and activities that cater to your negative values. Fill that vacuum with things that will nurture your positive values instead.
- Your flipflop values represent opportunity. Set yourself up for success by creating the chance for these values to come out in the best light.

If you notice a big discrepancy between what you currently value—what you spend most of your time and energy on—and what you'd like to value, know that you are not alone. Most of us do not walk the talk, at least not all of the time. But by going through this assessment, you have spotted your strengths and weaknesses, and given yourself a solid path to follow.

Allow yourself the time and resources to feed your treasured values. Align your actions with what's important to you. You will feel stronger and more at peace. You will find it easier to shrug off the petty concerns that used to fill you with anxiety and self-doubt. You will become a more confident, TOO Sexy you.

Take Stock of Your Skills

You are more than your personality and your values. You also have more skills than you realize. Take the time to list at least 10 things you're good at:

- At home
- With friends
- At work

We have the strange fortune of being able to access more information than any other people ever have in the history of mankind. That means we can compare ourselves to a mind-boggling number of people—dead or living. Yes, someone is always going to be more skilled than you in just about anything you can think of. But this exercise isn't about that. Comparisons don't matter. If you're good at something, write it down. End of story.

Track Your Social Capital

"No man is an island", declared the poet John Donne. Meaning, we all rely on each other. Each one of us has access to an extensive network of resources that we rely on—whether every day or one in a while. Often, we lose sight of just how extensive our social networks are. Taking the time to write down how much social capital you have can boost your confidence levels. Do it now. Take stock of:

- Your extended family.
- The people and places you can go to for a good time.
- People you can go to in an emergency (including close friends and family, as well as strangers in the community who would be there to help you).

- People and places that can help you meet your spiritual needs.
- Professional connections.
- Any clubs or groups you belong to.
- Public spaces where you can hang out such as parks.
- Places where you can enlarge your mind, such as museums, libraries, and free university lectures.

Be Thankful

So far, this chapter has been all about you. I want you to be full of self-approval on your path to a TOO Sexy you. But appreciating the amazing resources and network around you is important, too. When you focus on the things you lack—how you're not good enough at this; how you don't have enough of that—it's easy to feel down on yourself and the world. The opposite is also true: when you are aware of the bounty of things that are right in your life, it's easier to feel fortunate and content.

You've probably met very religious people who have an aura of sunniness around them. Little can dent their armor of tranquility. Regardless of your religious beliefs, you can share a similar experience. Taking time each day to take note of all that you have to be grateful for helps you realize you have a life of abundance. When things don't go your way, it's easier to take, because you know all the things that are slanted in your favor. And that makes it easier to be more confident and... yup, TOO Sexy.

Chapter Review: Revealing truths that you never knew were in you:

- Knowing why you lack confidence isn't enough; you have to give yourself plenty of reasons to feel sexy about yourself.

- Sometimes others can see assets in you that you can't see yourself. Listen to your friends.

- A values inventory can show you what factors are currently important in your life, and which factors should be.

- Aligning your action with your positive values will lead to a more self-assured, relaxed you. And that's TOO Sexy.

- Taking the time each day to count your blessings lets you realize how much you have going for you.

5. BRINGING SEXY BACK

If you're like most people, you've been nodding along as you read this book. You've seen the harm of the TOO factor in action, you've felt the media's effects on your self-esteem, and you've seen confident TOO sexy people who seem to rise above it all. You knew instantly who the toxic people in your life are, you had a good idea which TV shows are most damaging to your self-worth, and you found yourself smiling at the thought of a song that makes your soul soar. And yet, chances are you're still your old TOO caught up, TOO judgmental self.

If you've already made big changes, congratulations—your TOO sexy life is just around the corner. But, if you're like most people, all you've done is taken a few half-measures. Maybe you thought about some things you like about yourself, but didn't bother to stick them on the mirror. Maybe you thought about having an uncomfortable conversation with a so-called friend, but figured now was not the right time. And you've probably noticed that this hasn't made much of a difference in how you feel. Sure, it helps to understand what's going on behind how people act, but just knowing isn't enough. If you want to stop feeling like you're not good enough, you need to start taking action—in a big way.

You probably know that. So why aren't you doing anything about it? Because DOING feels too hard. As amazing as it may sound, you've grown comfortable with your unhappiness. You know what to expect from the life you currently live, even if you don't care for parts of it. Changing seems exciting, but more than that, it seems difficult. And changing into someone sexy and confident may appear downright alien and scary. You're in good company feeling this way—which is why so many people stay in jobs they hate or relationships that drain them. You could read self-help book after book and be an expert in theory, **without your life becoming one bit better.** You wouldn't be the first person.

Excuses, Excuses

Here are some common excuses people use to justify their inaction—and my responses. Whether you want to invoke ancient Greek (Carpe Diem) or one of the most successful brands in the world (Just Do It) the bottom line is the same.

"My life isn't that bad." Don't kid yourself. Sure, there are people out there who have it worse, but that's no reason to start working on making your life better right now. If looking at yourself in the mirror makes your stomach wrench. If the idea of shopping for clothes or meeting up with "the gang" makes you break out in sweat. If you ever binge on ice cream to stop from feeling bad about how you look. Then you **deserve** to start making your life better RIGHT NOW.

The fact that things aren't "that bad" actually works in your favor. That means you have resources—good friends, some degree of self-confidence, enough energy—to take thing to the next level. Use what you have as the foundation to make more. Don't wait until your life is so bad that you can't see a way to change even if you're desperate to do so.

"It's not a good time." – Things are too busy at work. You're going through a rocky time in a relationship. Or maybe you're in the midst of major family issues. Honestly, it's never a good time—until you make it one. Yes, it's true that some of the suggestions in this book require much time and energy, but most of them are small steps that you can act on RIGHT NOW. How long will it take you to write down five things you love about yourself every week? How long to read them in the mirror? And when you bother to figure out what TV shows to cut out, you will suddenly find you have much more time to work on the most important project of your life—yourself! Just start taking those steps—EVERY DAY! Once you start going and allow yourself to make a habit out of taking care of yourself, you will see how easy it is. In fact, it will make whatever else is going on in your life easier to handle. Don't wait until you find yourself looking back at your life with regret. Act NOW!

"I don't know where to start." – No ONE thing brought you to the point you are today, and no ONE thing is going to fix it. But a plan with too many moving parts can feel overwhelming. I will talk about goal-setting in further detail in Chapter 7. For now, start by spelling out all the sexy things about you. Write them out. Write them twice—once on a sticky note, and once in your Too Sexy journal (which you can find in Chapter 6 of the print version, or which you can buy for yourself if you're reading this as an ebook). Once you've knocked that out, go back to the end of Chapter 1 and come up with quips to handle any TOO factor insult anyone throws at you. Then make your way through each of the steps in Chapter 2 and 3.

You don't need to do everything at once. In fact, you don't want to! Binging on anything—even ways to boost your self-esteem—is no good, and it's not the way to make a life-long change. You want to hit the problem from as many angles as possible, over time, and you want to build up the solution the same way. THAT creates staying power to a TOO Sexy you. So give yourself permission to work on one thing at a time —as long as you're always working and moving forward.

"I'm not good enough." - This is a reason most people barely dare whisper to themselves, let alone say aloud. It's a reason people cloak in excuses, sometimes layers of excuses. It's a reason that makes my heart break. It's the reason I wrote the book in the first place—because I cannot stand the idea of people feeling like they're not good enough just because someone somewhere wanted to line their pockets with more money. Those actions have unleashed an unrealistic thought: it's best to fit a mold. Those cutting comments your grandmother made when you were growing up, the schoolyard jeers, the dark thoughts you have in the dressing room, all added fuel to that fire. Funny thing is, the mold is impossible to fit.

I am dedicating the rest of this chapter to dealing with the idea that you're not good enough. But the bottom line is that while you may have all sorts of "reasons" why you haven't started on your TOO Sexy path, none of them are valid. There is one huge reason to start right now, though: You DESERVE to spend the rest of your life feeling confident and happy. Enough said.

Meet Your Worse Enemy

You are already aware of all the land-mines out there—the media advertising, even so-called friends. But one important individual is missing from that list— you!

We are used to relying on our minds. From making small talk to getting your work done, your mind is your biggest resource. You trust it. But maybe you shouldn't —not completely at any rate. Your mind can lie, even to itself.

You've probably heard friends complaining about their looks—they're too fat, their hair is all wrong, their faces look awful. And most of the time you can look those friends straight in the face and ask, "What are they talking about?" Sure, you have friends that could look better, and friends who are perpetually fishing for compliments. But most of the time, your friends are voicing a real doubt, one that exists only in their heads. Everyone else can see they're great. Why can't they?

Or how about the friend who keeps making lame excuses for her boyfriend's horrible behavior. How can she be so blind? And the friend who always ignores constructive criticism, so much so that nobody even bothers anymore? In other words, you've seen plenty of evidence that people can lie to themselves. You are not the exception to this rule.

It's frightening to realize that you can be betrayed by your own mind. But it can also be liberating. If your mind can lie, then maybe all your negative self-talk is not true. "You're not good enough to..." "You'll never...." "You can't..." "You look..." It's not true.

Repeat. It's not true. And you can call your mind on it. You can stop the self-criticism cold and say to yourself "You are too biased about your looks, so I'm not going to listen to you about this anymore."

Try it. Next time you notice that your thoughts are putting you down, say "I trust you about this," and move on. Yes, it can be hard to wrestle control back from your brain, especially about lies you've been telling yourself for years. But are you really going to do nothing except continue to make yourself miserable?

Choose to take charge instead. You will be surprised at how easy it is—once you realize that you have control over you. And when you quiet your inner critic, your confidence level will naturally go up. And you know what that means. A Too Sexy you.

Letting Go of Perfectionism

Not only can your mind steer you wrong, but it can get worked up over nothing. Remember how traumatic shots used to be when you were a kid? Sure, they're no fun, but they're also not worth hyperventilating about. For a lot of kids, the prelude to the shot—what their minds do to themselves—is considerably worse, and lasts considerably longer than the shot itself. And don't forget the shadows in your room that used to keep you up night after night even though you never had any proof that something was there?

Even today, your mind might be conjuring up another bogeyman—the idea that if you're not perfect, you're not good enough. If you're not a perfectionist, congratulations for dodging that bullet. But if you are, here are three ugly truths that you must face about your perfectionist ways:

Perfectionism is impossible. Remember when we went over how much effort and manipulation goes into those "ideal" bodies? How you set yourself up for failure and disappointment when you try to reach the unreachable? Perfectionism, in general, is like that. Yes, you can occasionally do things perfectly, and yes, it's always a good idea to do your best. But expecting perfection every time leads to self-criticism, stress, and depression—NOT to perfection.

Perfectionism takes too much effort. Yes, some people have to do some things perfectly. Brain surgery comes to mind. But in most cases, the quest for perfection is not only futile, but exhausting. Think about how much effort it takes to go from what most people would find "good enough" to "perfect".

Closing that gap between good enough and perfect takes a great deal of time and energy—time and energy that you could be using in a better way. And then, either you fail to reach your absurdly high standard, or you reach it, and fail to be adequately appreciated for it.

Perfectionism can hurt your relationships. Or maybe, you just spend the rest of your time obsessing about keeping things perfect, to the extent that you alienate your friends and loved ones.

I have a friend who always cleans house before she invites friends over. She believes it's easier to feel at ease in a tidy, inviting house. People often comment on the look and feel of her house, as they lean back and sip their drinks. If you look closely enough, you might see cobwebs in the corner or spots on the window. But it doesn't matter—her mission's been accomplished.

Another friend keeps a spotless house. People are intimidated about asking her over because they know they can't possibly meet her high standards. But they don't enjoy going to her house either. They spend the entire time worrying about tracking dirt or spilling crumbs. She cleans up behind everyone, washes dishes before people are done digesting, and generally, just transfers her uptight feelings to her guests. Not cool. Imagine how much better things would be if she just kept her house neat and relaxed with her guests.

Face it. Far from being an ideal, the quest for perfectionism can be not only futile, but detrimental. It wrecks your confidence. And your neurotic tendencies and inability to be satisfied with yourself are the opposite of sexy. You owe it to yourself to learn to be happy with good enough. Follow these steps to start toning down your need for perfection:

1. Figure out what drives your need for perfectionism.. Love and acceptance are usually root causes.

2. Test the logic behind your beliefs. I started that process for you above, but you may need to go further.

3. List the pros and cons of your perfectionism. In the back of your mind, you've known all along that there are costs, but chances are you never let yourself examine all of them. Now's your chance.

4. Practice honest thinking.

The last step can be the trickiest one. It goes back to what I mentioned earlier: your mind can lie to you. When you fall short of perfection, your brain automatically generates negative thoughts— "I'm not good enough," "I should have tried harder," "Everyone will think I'm a loser." You have to train yourself to realize that these thoughts are NOT reality. In fact, many of them stem from "all or nothing" thinking: either you get it perfect, or you're worthless. Nothing could be further from the truth. Between black and white lie not only countless shades of grey, but all the colors of the rainbow.

Chances are, you don't expect perfection from your friends and loved ones. You appreciate them warts and all. Trust them to be able to do the same for you. And give yourself the same leeway you give them. When your mind says "Not good enough," give yourself permission to say "Actually, it is," and move on to the next thing.

Once you let go of your perfectionism, you will find your anxieties will decrease, your level of relaxation will soar, and it will be so much easier to feel confident and TOO Sexy.

Fake It Until You Make It

What if perfectionism isn't your problem? What if you "know" you're so far from perfect that there's no point in even aiming for it. Your problem isn't always trying to reach for too-high standards. It's that your self-esteem is in shambles. Again, the key is in realizing that your mind lies to you and that either/or thinking simply isn't true. While you work on creating healthier, more honest thoughts, there's much you can do on the outside, too.

You've probably seen one of those reality shows where someone is performing before a huge live audience—not to mention millions of TV viewers—for the first time. You see them pacing beforehand, wringing their hands. Then they get on stage, walk up to the mic, and let pure magic pour out of their voices. It's amazing to see an amateur acting like they've been doing something professionally for years. What's their secret? Are they immune to nerves? Of course not. Are they a natural-performer? Maybe. But what does that mean?

Another word for performer is actor. Performing before an audience, then, means putting on the show they're expecting to see. It has NOTHING to do with what the performer feels on the inside. And these amazingly talented people often fall apart as soon as the song is over—no matter how well they were doing. In fact, sometimes the better they did, the bigger the wreck they are afterwards. They're NOT pros; they haven't learned to take things in stride. But they do such a good job of acting the part when it counts that they get swept up in their own performance.

The ability to present a different image on the outside than you feel on the inside is literally a million-dollar skill. And it's one you can do, too. All those years of negative messages about your TOO factors aren't going to go away overnight just because you're ready for them to. You're not going to wake up tomorrow feeling uber-confident and TOO Sexy. But what you CAN do tomorrow—or even this very moment—is ACT confident and powerful. Fake it until you make it. Look on the outside how you want to feel on the inside. You'll be amazed at the effect it has.

One of the biggest fears doctors have is malpractice suits. You'd think boning up on medicine and making the best diagnosis and treatment decisions possible would be the most important thing a doctor can do to avoid ending up in court. Those things certainly help. But what matters the most is bedside matter—how doctors treat patients on a personal level. If you're sick and the person who's supposed to be making you better is a world-class jerk, you're not going to be very happy with their care. It's that simple.

Except, for some docs, it's not simple at all. Many people go into medicine because they're very smart and love learning and being challenged. Some of these same people are not very good at interacting with other humans. They might be super awkward or they might be offensive. But the smart ones put on a show —they ACT like they're the smoothest, most interested person. Sure, you might be able to tell the difference between the doc acting and the doc who really has great people skills, but you can tell the bigger difference between the doc acting and the one who doesn't bother. The later one is going to have quite the bumpy career. But the ones who go through the motions find it easier and easier to say and do the right things, until they become masters at putting patients and their families at ease. Doing that doesn't just make them better humans, and less prone to lawsuits; it also makes them better doctors. Patients who think their doctors care get better faster than ones who don't. The placebo effect is a powerful thing.

You can harness its power yourself. Remember that the majority of human communication in real life is nonverbal. The way you stand, the way you look—or don't look—at someone leak information about how you feel. Here are four simple steps to appearing more confident, regardless of how you feel inside:

- **Take care of your appearance.** What?! Hasn't this whole book been about the fact that we're too obsessed—in the wrong ways—with how we look? Absolutely. I'm not saying you should aspire to some unrealistic ideal. I AM saying that you should leave your house with your face washed, teeth cleaned, hair brushed, and clothes looking like you didn't pick it off the floor. It's much easier to fake confidence when you don't look slovenly. It's also much easier to feel confidence when you don't feel like you need to apologize for how you look.

- **Stand tall.** This isn't about gaining a couple of inches of height. It's about good posture. You would be amazed what slumped shoulders and a slouch convey about someone. On the other hand, walking with your back straight and your shoulders back shows the world that you are confident—even if you're not. Good posture is just as important when you're on your derriere. Remember to sit up, too.

- **Maintain eye contact.** You're not out to win staring contests; that will just make other people feel uncomfortable or, worse, creep them out. You do, however, want to appear confident enough that you can look anybody in the eye, whether it be for a friendly greeting or during high-powered negotiations. The importance of eye-contact is genetically hard-wired into us. Looking down or casting your eyes sideways shows submission, which is another way of saying that you're not as good as the person you're talking to. So get in the habit of looking people in the eye; just remember that staring is not polite.

- **Smile.** A smile may be one of the most powerful tools known to man. Even babies master it by the time they are two months old—long before seemingly important things like being able to eat solid foods or move around. A genuine smile lets other people know you are friendly and approachable, and feel good about yourself and others around you. Try it. If you don't feel like smiling, force it. Just the ACT of smiling will lift your mood, and the reaction you get from others will keep you going.

You might have to keep reminding yourself to do these four things, but they're not hard. Soon they will become second nature—if you let them! But the amazing thing is how powerful they are. When you have good posture and approach people with friendly interest, they will treat you like the confident person they think you are. And when you start noticing the difference in how people treat you, it will grow your self-confidence and your inner sexiness. In other words, just like with the reality shows—faking it actually helps you make it.

Seeking Outside Help

It's almost impossible to grow up in our society without developing hang-ups, sometimes major ones. A certain level of anxiety and self-doubt is normal, and can be overcome with some effort. But sometimes our problems are bigger than we can handle by ourselves.

If you:

- Find your existence painful on a regular basis
- Self-medicate using drugs or alcohol (for instance, drink to forget or to go numb)
- Can see no reason to live or wish you were dead
- Are actively planning out suicide

Then please seek help. Talk to your health care provider, counselor, or clergyman. Call a crisis hotline number. There is no shame in getting help, and you owe it to yourself to do so.

People often think their problem is not "dramatic" enough to justify seeking help. But if you find that you can't handle something on your own—from general worries to social anxieties to self-esteem issues—then please seek help. With help, you CAN feel better about yourself and start on your path to a confident, TOO Sexy you.

Hate the Game, Don't Be a Player

On your road to sexiness, remember one thing: confidence does not equal cattiness. You are TOO sexy for backtalk! We all know how it feels to be on the receiving end of insults. But how many times have you made snap judgments about other people's TOO factors? Too nerdy, too fat, too ugly, too lame, too short, too skinny, too something. Admit it—you're guilty as charged. Even as we get hurt by other's unrealistic expectations, we perpetuate the cycle ourselves. And that has to stop.

Being TOO sexy means being above the need to judge others. Remember, everyone has a backstory. A friend of mine remembers meeting a huge patient at a hospital who easily weighed almost 400 pounds. She could not believe how large he had allowed himself to get, until she heard his story. He had actually tipped the scales around 800 pounds, and had since lost half his body weight. Though his struggles were hardly over, he had accomplished an incredible feat.

My friend says meeting this man shocked her into noticing how critical and narrow-minded she could be —even as she struggled with accepting her own TOO factors. Even if he hadn't been through this journey, she realized it was not her role to project her insecurities and value judgments on others.

It is one thing to be a friend—to point out potential health risks such as excessive drinking, and to support people who are asking for help in bettering themselves. It is another to assume we know all we need to about someone because of the way they don't fit into the too-narrow boxes society has imposed on us. When you find yourself thinking snidely about others—and you will, it's only natural—make the conscious decision to be better than that. You don't need to put others down to feel good about yourself. You're TOO sexy for that.

Chapter Review: Getting on the Right Track

- Be a doer, not a thinker. Changing yourself takes effort - but it's worth it.

- It may be cliché, but you're your own worst enemy. Don't let you brain get you down.

- Don't strive for perfection. It's almost always unattainable.

- Fake confidence until you leave it.

- And remember, it's easier to act the part if you look it. Dress (and wash) accordingly.

- Don't be a hypocrite. Put aside preconceptions and treat people the way you'd want to be treated.

6. DIARY OF A "TOO" SEXY INDIVIDUAL

This chapter is just for you. Diary, journal, notebook. It doesn't matter what you call it, just that you use it. You can jot down clever comebacks, list all your won- derful attributes, or spell out what beauty means to you. Use this space to take notes whenever a particular part of this book strikes a chord. You can chronicle your trials and your triumphs, or write down your plans for the future. In fact, forget about that "or." Do it all. When you run out of space here, buy a journal that in- vites you to put your pen to paper. Or create a blog, if that's more your style. Regardless of the format, the more you write, the better off you will be.

Why write? Here are six terrific reasons for you to get started:

1. Change doesn't just happen; it occurs in stages. In the first stage, you may sense that something's wrong, but the need for change isn't even on your radar. Then you're thinking about it. Buying and reading through this book was part of the next stage. But reading takes considerably less effort

than doing. Writing is a good way to bridge the gap into acting. In other words, putting your thoughts down on paper helps build your ability to turn into a more confident you.

2. Writing brings the emotional and the logical (wordy) side of your brain together, forcing you to face up to your feelings. At the same time, it helps you think more rationally, the first step to truly working through your problems.

3. Your brain can only hold a list of about seven things at a time. You're going to need to record a lot of things—all the great aspects of your looks, your personality, and your actions. Don't let them slip from your mind—make them permanent!

4. The more senses you can employ, the better off your memory will be. Actively writing, then occasionally reading back your own words will those positive messages about yourself sink in.

5. You are embarking on a grand journey. You owe it to yourself to keep a record of your thoughts, feelings, troubles, and victories along the way.

6. Making a habit of writing means making a habit of thinking in a TOO Sexy way. Remember, you have a lifetime of negative messages to overcome. The more time and thought you spend on it, the more naturally feeling and acting TOO Sexy will be.

What are you waiting for? Get ready. Get set. Write! Your TOO Sexy self is waiting.

TOO SEXY

TOO SEXY

7. ON YOUR MARK, TOO SEXY, GO!

I hope this book has led you along a path of self-discovery. You have faced some ugly truths about society, your friends, and yourself. You know the insecurities society has instilled in you—and why. You are aware of how your own mind can lie that you're not good enough. You have obtained a clear picture of who you are now—your media-imposed "flaws", your real faults, and your abundance of strengths. You are taking baby-steps toward a new, TOO Sexy you.

But you may still be feeling far from that confident, head-turning person you wish to be. That is okay. You have the tools—from this book, inside yourself, and with the help of friends and mentors—to do it.

How to Change - Permanently

Change is not an on-off switch; it doesn't just happen. Researchers have discovered that we must go through stages before we can transform into our better selves. Knowing these stages helps both in understanding your own journey, and appreciating what others have to go through. For instance, if you know someone who might benefit from the lessons in this book, do not be surprised or hurt if they are not receptive to it. Their current stage may just be different than yours.

Pre-contemplation is your infant stage. It's where you are before you realize anything is wrong. Next comes contemplating the need for change. It is the "should I?" stage. In the third stage, you ask "How should I?" You prepare by reading books, talking to friends, asking expert opinions, and perhaps buying resources. Depending on their personality and level of interest, people stay at the contemplation stage for different amounts of time. Remember, educating yourself is important, but at some point, you need to act.

The action stage is fourth. Here, you create the change you sought. When this action becomes habit— when you act not to change, but to maintain your new stage, you have reached the last stage, the stage that will hopefully last a lifetime. Many people do not manage a permanent change, however. Instead they relapse and must renew the cycle. This chapter is about helping you avoid that. All you have to do is keep moving forward on the path you are on.

Set Goals

Studies have shown that people who set specific, tangible goals are much more likely to change—and stay changed—than people who have vague wishes. Yet, years of failed New Year's Resolutions, diets, etc. have shown us that goals rarely pan out. What makes the difference between success and failure? Here are six things you can do to ensure that you will stick to your goals and see them through.

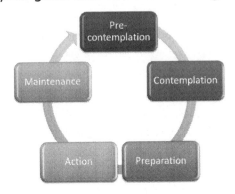

1. **Believe in yourself.** How many times have you "committed" to something knowing you were likely to fail. And when you did... well, you knew it all along, right? That's called the self-fulfilling prophecy, and it's as detrimental as it is common. Change cannot happen unless you will it to be so. It's like Yoda says, "Do, or do not. There is no try." Do not try to be sexier... just be it. I can hear some of you now, "But I can't," "I don't know how." Actually, you can. I set up this book to show you the traps people make for themselves and each other, in order for you to avoid them. Then I asked you to do a handful of exercises to build up your reservoir of wonderful. I let you know what sort of people are harmful to your cause, and which ones can be helpful. In other words, you have all the tools you need—inside you and around you—to make real change. You CAN do it. But your first step is to believe.

2. **Believe in your goal.** All those years of being torn down, laughed at, and second-guessed make you question yourself. It's only natural. You may even be at a point where you're thinking "I don't care what people think. I don't need to prove myself to anyone." This is not be a bad point of view—except if you are feeling bitter, resentful, or insecure when you think it. When you can't get what you want, your brain protects you by pretending you don't really care, even though it's obvious you do. So, you might have to convince yourself that at some level you do care what people think, and you want them to see you in a positive light—just on your terms. It's okay to admit that there's something missing from your life.

Nothing's wrong with wanting to be wanted. We are social creatures, after all. We are genetically and culturally wired to want to belong. Feeling sexy and confident are worthwhile goals. They will make you feel better about yourself, about each day, about how to interact with others. You will feel more energetic and powerful. And more people will be drawn to you. But none of this matters unless you believe it's a worthwhile goal. If you want to be free of negative perceptions and be full of confidence and sexiness, you have to WANT IT bad enough to work on it.

3. **Build a ladder.** Being TOO Sexy sounds like a great goal, but it suffers one huge problem: it's too vague. You need to figure out what being Too Sexy would mean to you. Maybe you want the self-assurance to hold your head high all day. Maybe you want to genuinely smile at the reflection in the mirror. Maybe you want the confidence to talk in front of a crowd. Define your goal in a way that lets you know whether you've achieved it or not.

4. **Create subgoals**. The harder or further away your end goal seems, the more steps you will want to give yourself. Achieving milestones will give you confidence in your ability to move in the right direction and ultimately achieve your goals. Your milestones might look something like this:

> 1. I will write five things I like about myself every week.
> 2. I will repeat those five things out loud every time I look in the mirror.

3.I will learn comebacks for when people make me feel bad about my "flaws."

4.I will put a break to every lie I catch my brain telling me.

5.I will walk tall, make eye contact and smile to a stranger every time I go to the store—no matter how I feel inside.

6.I will walk tall, make eye contact, and smile every day.

Look at step 5 an 6. See how you can build on your goals incrementally? It's like going from not exercising, to exercising for 15 minutes three times a week, to through a series of gradual improvements, exercising for an hour five days a week.

5. **Make a public commitment**. Don't just tell yourself you are going to change, announce it to the world. Tell people who can act as cheerleaders when you do well, and people who will tease you if you fail. Take advantage of peer pressure by committing yourself in a way that will make failing embarrassing. Update your supporters on your progress—in person or through Facebook or Twitter posts.

6. **Accept setbacks.** It would be wonderful if you met every goal every time, but life often doesn't work that way. Rather than seeing yourself in black-and-white terms as a success or failure, you need to realize that struggling is part of the process. You need to remember that "a slip is not a fall." If you binge on reality shows one day or feel down on yourself about your looks, that doesn't mean you've failed or

that you can't be TOO Sexy. All it means is you had a bad day. Tomorrow is a new one. Don't use setbacks as excuses to quit because you're not good enough. Just reaffirm your beliefs in your goals and in yourself, check to make sure that your milestones are realistic, and keep going.

Reward Yourself

Don't just note your achievements, celebrate them. What is an achievement? It's when you do something that's a big deal to you, regardless of whether it is to anyone else.

I have a friend who thought nothing of things that other people found difficult, like acing her law school entrance exams. Yet, running—okay, jogging—was tremendously challenging for her. I jogged with her a few times, and she would collapse in a mass of sweat afterwards. Not pretty. But when she finally managed to be able to run a mile, and then keep walking afterwards, it was a BIG deal. She eventually worked up to two miles... and then three. It was never fast or particularly graceful, but she did it—and she was rightfully proud. Scoring a great job? That was nice. But crossing the finish line? That was huge.

Think of your achievements the same way. You don't need to pat your back for things that other people think matter—only for what's meaningful to you. If making eye contact is hard for you, then make a big deal out of it when you do. Or cutting down on trashy TV. Or decreasing the amount of self-criticism. Take ownership of your successes and celebrate them accordingly.

Taking time to do this is important. First, it helps you realize what you've achieved. Second, it helps make the process fun. Finally, it serves as an incentive to achieve more. But you have to reward yourself the right way. Too often, we rely on two types of prizes: food and stuff. Both can be self-defeating. If you applaud your new level of confidence by splurging on the hottest new outfit, you might just be feeding into the cycle that those corporate fat cats started. On the other hand, if you indulge with desserts, you might end up feeling weak-willed afterwards. You'd be surprised how many people reward themselves in ways that make them backslide.

Plan ahead to give yourself appropriate rewards. Make your celebration fit with your goals and your values. Instead of having a TV marathon, curl up on the couch with a good book. Enjoy a high-end meal instead of a carton of ice cream. Treat yourself to a day at the beach or the park instead of at the mall. In other words, do make your rewards work for you, instead of serving as sabotage.

Enjoy The Journey

We are one of the most impatient societies in the history of mankind. How many people do you know who find the microwave annoyingly slow, or their high-speed internet? We want instant gratification—thanks yet again, corporate big wigs. But, like that old Heinz commercial went, the best things come to those who wait.

You have embarked on a huge undertaking. Whether that means writing about it, trying things you've never done before, or sharing your experiences with like-minded people, enjoy the process. Don't trade the stress of thinking you're not good enough regarding some "flaw" for the stress of not achieving your goals fast enough. It's not worth it. Instead of being in a rush to be perfectly confident and sexy, take this opportunity to learn about yourself and to note all your daily triumphs, however small. Don't focus so much on what you lack, and pay more attention to what you are achieving. That's the road to greater confidence and a TOO sexy you.

Hello, Success

Congratulations on reaching the end of the book—and the beginning of a lifetime as a TOO sexy you. Each one of us must go through our own personal journey, yet we can learn from each other. Continue to find strength and ideas from every circumstance regardless of the feeling it gives you initially. Please email me at stan@stanpearson.com to let me know your story. What led you to pick up this book? What Too factor or factors were causing your problems? How have the lessons from this book impacted you already? What are your TOO sexy plans for the future? Use the power of your voice to make a difference and share a positive, more empowered, better version of you.

ABOUT THE AUTHOR

Stan Pearson II, is a Speaker, Motivational Comedian, Host, Actor & Author who uses comedy, interactive activities and real life easy to apply expertise to connect to his audience. He has a BA in Spanish and earned his MBA as well. Because of his ready smile, you might think Stan leads a perfect life, but we all also understand nothing is perfect which creates a life of better understanding for all of us. He saw himself, sisters and friends always accused of being "TOO" something or not enough of something else. He launched the TOO Sexy movement to push everyone to be better today than they were yesterday -- by making it easier for everyone to have fun and feel good about themselves. We have to find our sexy from the inside out.

Stan's books, presentations & private coaching groups connect, entertain and educate everyone regardless of race, cultural or socio-economic backgrounds. If you are looking for a speaker or host who is engaging, interactive, charismatic & funny; Stan is your man.

MOTIVATE AND INSPIRE OTHERS!

BOOK ME TO SPEAK
TO YOUR ORGANIZATION, SCHOOL, BUSINESS OR MASTERMIND

"SHARE THIS BOOK"

SPECIAL QUANTITY DISCOUNTS

5- 20 Books	$15.95
21-99 Books	$14.95
100-499 Books	$13.95
500-999 Books	$11.95
1000+ Books	$8.95

TO PLACE AN ORDER CONTACT:
888.498.7826
STAN@STANPEARSON.COM

#FINDYOURSEXY
#AMITOOSEXY
#EVERYDAYSEXY
#CONTROLYOURFEED

41766113R00063